LOS ANGELES
Lakers

BY K. C. KELLEY

Published by The Child's World®
1980 Lookout Drive • Mankato, MN 56003-1705
800-599-READ • www.childsworld.com

Acknowledgments
The Child's World®: Mary Berendes, Publishing Director
Red Line Editorial: Editorial direction
The Design Lab: Design
Amnet: Production

Design elements: PhotoDisc, Viorika Prikhodko/
iStockphoto

Photographs ©: Sue Ogrocki/AP Images, cover, title;
Mark J. Terrill/AP Images, 5, 10; David J. Phillip/AP
Images, 6; AP Images, 9; Kevin Reece/AP Images, 13;
Michael Conroy/AP Images, 17; Chris Carlson/AP
Images, 18; Lee Celano/AP Images, 21; Mark Lennihan/
AP Images, 22; Daniel Johnston/AP Images, 25, 26

ISBN 978-1623235000
LCCN 2013931367

Printed in the United States of America
Mankato, MN
July, 2013
PA02171

About the Author

K. C. Kelley has written dozens
of books on basketball, football,
baseball, and other sports for
young readers. K. C. used to
work for NFL Publishing and has
covered several Super Bowls.
He likes to watch any basketball
game, but the Los Angeles Lakers
are his favorite team.

Table *of* Contents

4 Go, Lakers!

7 Who Are the Lakers?

8 Where They Came From

11 Who They Play

12 Where They Play

15 The Basketball Court

16 Big Days

19 Tough Days

20 Meet the Fans

23 Heroes Then . . .

24 Heroes Now . . .

27 Gearing Up

28 *Sports Stats*

30 *Glossary*

31 *Find Out More*

32 *Index*

Go, Lakers!

The Los Angeles Lakers play basketball in a city where movies are made. The Lakers put on an amazing show themselves! They have star players like films have movie stars. They win big games like movies win big awards. And like movies, the Lakers have millions of fans! Let's find out more about this awesome collection of shining basketball stars.

Kobe Bryant is the star of today's Lakers.

Who Are the Lakers?

The Los Angeles Lakers play in the National Basketball Association (NBA). They are one of 30 teams in the NBA. The NBA includes the Eastern Conference and the Western Conference. The Lakers play in the Pacific Division of the Western Conference. The winner of the Eastern Conference plays the winner of the Western Conference in the **NBA Finals**. The Lakers have been the NBA champions 16 times—the second-most ever!

Kobe Bryant celebrates the Lakers' NBA title in 2009.

Where They Came From

The Lakers first played in 1947–48. They played in Minneapolis at the time. The team moved to Los Angeles in 1960. The first Lakers team played in the National Basketball League (NBL). Then the Lakers joined the Basketball Association of America (BAA) in 1948–49. That league joined with another to become the NBA after that. The Lakers were league champions in six of their first seven years! Then, from 1959 to 1970, they made it to the NBA Finals eight times. But they lost all eight. Seven of those losses came against the Boston Celtics.

Center George Mikan (in dark) was the Lakers' biggest star when they played in Minneapolis.

Who They Play

The Lakers play 82 games each season. That's a lot of basketball! They play every other NBA team at least once each season. They play teams in their division and conference more often. Since the 1960s, the Lakers have had a big **rivalry** with the Boston Celtics. Those two teams have often battled in the NBA Finals. The Lakers also play against another NBA team in Los Angeles, the Clippers.

The Celtics and Lakers have long been cross-country rivals.

Where They Play

The Lakers play their home games at the Staples Center. This large indoor arena holds approximately 19,000 people for Lakers games. The team moved into this home in 1999. The Staples Center is also home to the Clippers. It also is the home of the National Hockey League's Los Angeles Kings. The Staples Center hosts rock concerts, skateboard shows, and lots of other events, too.

The court at the Staples Center can be changed from Lakers colors to Clippers colors.

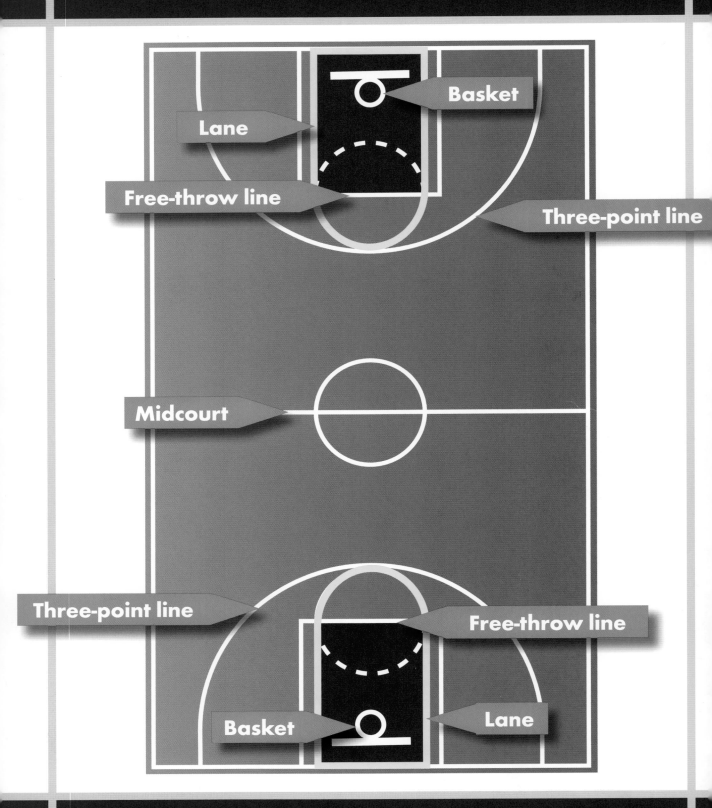

Basket

Lane

Free-throw line

Three-point line

Midcourt

Three-point line

Free-throw line

Basket

Lane

The Basketball Court

Basketball is played on a court made of wood. An NBA court is 94 feet (29 m) long. A painted line shows the middle of the court. Other lines lay out the free-throw area. The space below each basket is known as the "lane." The baskets at each end are 10 feet (3 m) off the ground. The metal rims of the baskets stick out over the court. Nylon nets hang from the rims.

Big Days

The Los Angeles Lakers have had many great moments in their long history. Here are three of the greatest:

1949: The Minneapolis Lakers won their first NBA championship. It was the start of a streak of five titles in six years.

1972: During the season, the Los Angeles Lakers won a record 33 games in a row. They went on to win their first NBA title since 1954. It was their first title since moving to Los Angeles.

2010: The Lakers won their sixteenth NBA title. Coach Phil Jackson set an NBA record by winning his eleventh title (he won six of them while coaching the Chicago Bulls).

Kobe Bryant (left) and Shaquille O'Neal (right) led the Lakers to three titles as teammates.

Tough Days

The Lakers can't win all their games. Some games or seasons don't turn out well. The players keep trying to play their best, though. Here are some of the toughest seasons in Lakers history:

1958: The Lakers won only 19 games and lost 53. This was just four years after they were NBA champs in 1954.

2005: The Lakers missed the **playoffs**. It was one of just two seasons in which they missed the playoffs from 1977 through 2013.

2008: The Lakers battled their old rivals, the Boston Celtics, in the NBA Finals. The Celtics walloped the Lakers 131–92 in the final game to capture the title.

The Lakers had a rare down season in 2004–05.

Meet the Fans

Stars are everywhere at Lakers home games—not just on the basketball court! Many movie stars and famous musicians go to Lakers games. They sit very close to the court. Actor Jack Nicholson might be the Lakers' most dedicated fan. He has had courtside seats at Lakers games for many years. Many Lakers fans watch the movie and music stars as much as they watch the Lakers players.

Thousands showed up to the Lakers' 2001 victory party.

Heroes Then . . .

The Lakers have had superstars at every position—especially **center**. George Mikan was the NBA's first great center. He helped the Minneapolis Lakers win their first five NBA titles during the 1940s and 1950s. Another center, Wilt Chamberlain, led the Lakers to the 1972 championship. Kareem Abdul-Jabbar joined the Lakers in 1975. He scored more points than anyone else in NBA history! And center Shaquille O'Neal was the NBA Finals Most Valuable Player in 2000, 2001, and 2002. **Guard** Jerry West led the Lakers in the 1960s and 1970s. He had an awesome shooting touch. Then in the 1980s, guard Earvin "Magic" Johnson helped the Lakers win five more championships.

Earvin "Magic" Johnson (with ball) was a guard, but he could play any position.

Heroes Now . . .

Kobe Bryant is one of the best players in the NBA. He once scored 81 points in a game! He can make amazing leaps and **slam dunks**. He also can make a shot from just about anywhere. Bryant always seems to come through when his team really needs him most. **Forward** Pau Gasol certainly helps, though. He is from Spain. In 2012, Dwight Howard followed in the Lakers' long line of great centers. He is great at grabbing **rebounds**.

Few can score in the NBA like Kobe Bryant.

Arm sleeve

Jersey

Shorts

Socks

Basketball shoes

Gearing Up

Los Angeles Lakers players wear the team's uniform and special basketball sneakers. Some wear other pads to protect themselves. Check out this picture of Pau Gasol and learn about what NBA players wear.

THE BASKETBALL

NBA basketballs are made of leather. Several pieces are held together with rubber edges. Inside the leather ball is a hollow ball of rubber. This is filled with air. The leather is covered with little bumps called "pebbles." The pebbles help players get a good grip on the ball. The basketball used in the Women's National Basketball Association (WNBA) is slightly smaller than the men's basketball.

Forward Pau Gasol is a steady presence under the basket.

Note: All numbers shown are through the 2012–13 season.

HIGH SCORERS

These players have scored the most points for the Lakers.

PLAYER	POINTS
Kobe Bryant	31,617
Jerry West	25,192

HELPING HAND

Here are Los Angeles' all-time leaders in **assists**.

PLAYER	ASSISTS
Magic Johnson	10,141
Jerry West	6,238

CLEANING THE BOARDS

Rebounds are a big part of the game. Here are the Lakers' best rebounders.

PLAYER	REBOUNDS
Elgin Baylor	11,463
Kareem Abdul-Jabbar	10,279

MOST THREE-POINT SHOTS MADE

Shots taken from behind a line about 23 feet (7 m) from the basket are worth three points. Here are the Lakers' best at these long-distance shots.

PLAYER	THREE-POINT BASKETS
Kobe Bryant	1,637
Derek Fisher	846

COACH

Who coached the Lakers to the most wins?

Phil Jackson, 610

assists passes to teammates that lead directly to making baskets

center a player (usually the tallest on the team) who plays close to the basket

forward one of two tall players who rebound and score near the basket

guard one of two players who set up plays, pass to teammates closer to the basket, and shoot from farther away

NBA Finals the seven-game NBA championship series, in which the champion must win four games

playoffs a series of games between 16 teams that decides which two teams will play in the NBA Finals

rebounds missed shots that bounce off the backboard or rim and are grabbed by another player

rivalry an ongoing competition between teams that play each other often, over a long time

slam dunks shots made by stuffing the basketball down in the hoop

BOOKS

Frisch, Aaron. *Los Angeles Lakers*. Mankato, MN: Creative Paperbacks, 2012.

Gilbert, Sara. *The Story of the Los Angeles Lakers*. Mankato, MN: Creative Paperbacks, 2011.

Hareas, John. *Championship Teams*. New York: Scholastic, 2010.

Osier, Dan. *Kobe Bryant*. New York: PowerKids Press, 2011.

Smallwood, John N. *Megastars*. New York: Scholastic, 2011.

WEB SITES

Visit our Web site for links about the Los Angeles Lakers and other NBA teams: **childsworld.com/links**

Note to Parents, Teachers, and Librarians: We routinely verify our Web links to make sure they are safe and active sites. So encourage your readers to check them out!

INDEX

Abdul-Jabbar, Kareem, 23, 29
assists, 28
Basketball Association of America (BAA), 8
basketball court diagram, 14
baskets, 15
Baylor, Elgin, 29
Boston Celtics, 8, 11, 19
Bryant, Kobe, 24, 28, 29
centers, 23, 24
Chamberlain, Wilt, 23
Chicago Bulls, 16
coaches, 16, 29
Eastern Conference, 7
fans, 4, 20, 23
Fisher, Derek, 29
forward, 24

free-throw area, 15
Gasol, Pau, 24, 27
guards, 23
history, 8, 12, 16, 19, 23
Howard, Dwight, 24
Jackson, Phil, 16, 29
Johnson, Earvin "Magic," 23, 28
lane, 15
Los Angeles Clippers, 11, 12
Los Angeles Kings, 12
Mikan, George, 23
Minneapolis Lakers, 8, 16, 23
National Basketball League (NBL), 8
National Hockey League, 12
NBA championships, 7, 8, 16, 19, 23

NBA Finals, 7, 8, 11, 19
Nicholson, Jack, 20
O'Neal, Shaquille, 23
Pacific Division, 7
playoffs, 19
rebounds, 24, 29
rivals, 11, 19
Spain, 24
Staples Center, 12
three-point shots, 29
uniforms, 27
West, Jerry, 23, 28
Western Conference, 7
Women's National Basketball Association (WNBA), 27
worst season, 19